For Caroline, Kaz and Clare
S.H.

First published 1998 by Walker Books Ltd
87 Vauxhall Walk, London SE11 5HJ

This edition published 1999

10 9 8 7 6 5 4 3 2 1

This selection © 1998 Michael Rosen
Illustrations © 1998 Sue Heap

Printed in Hong Kong

British Library Cataloguing in Publication Data
A catalogue record for this book is
available from the British Library.

ISBN 0-7445-6788-2 (hb)
ISBN 0-7445-6999-0 (pb)

The editor and publisher gratefully acknowledge permission to
reproduce the following copyright material:

John Agard: "So-So Joe" from No Hickory, No Dickory, No Dock
published by Viking 1991 and "Where Does Laughter Begin?" from
Laughter Is an Egg published by Viking 1990, reprinted by kind
permission of John Agard c/o Caroline Sheldon Literary Agency.
Tony Bradman: "I Can Put My Socks On" from A Kiss on the Nose,
reprinted by permission of William Heinemann. Richard Edwards:
"How?" from The Word Party published by Puffin 1987, reprinted by
permission of the author. Eleanor Farjeon: "Cats" from The Children's
Bells, reprinted by permission of David Higham Associates.
Michelle Magorian: "I Won't" from Waiting for My Shorts to Dry
published by Viking Kestrel 1989 © Michelle Magorian 1989, reprinted
by permission of Frederick Warne & Co. Spike Milligan: "Today I Saw a
Little Worm" © Spike Milligan 1959, 1961, 1963, reprinted by
permission of Spike Milligan Productions Ltd.

Grace Nichols: "Granny, Granny, Please Comb My Hair" from Come
On into My Tropical Garden published by A & C Black, reprinted by
permission of Curtis Brown Ltd., on behalf of Grace Nichols © 1988.
Jack Prelutsky: "I Am Running in a Circle" from New Kid on the Block,
reprinted by permission of William Heinemann Ltd. Michael Rosen:
"Nursery Crimes" © Michael Rosen 1985, reprinted by permission of
André Deutsch Children's Books, an imprint of Scholastic Ltd. Clive
Sansom: "The Dustman" from Speech Rhymes, reprinted by permission
of A & C Black Ltd. Ian Serraillier: "The Tickle Rhyme" from The
Monster Horse © 1950 published by Oxford University Press, reprinted
by permission of Anne Serraillier.

While every effort has been made to obtain permission, there may still
be cases in which we have failed to trace a copyright holder, and we
would like to apologize for any apparent negligence.

NIGHT-NIGHT, KNIGHT

And Other Poems

Chosen by **Michael Rosen**

Illustrated by **Sue Heap**

WALKER BOOKS
AND SUBSIDIARIES
LONDON • BOSTON • SYDNEY

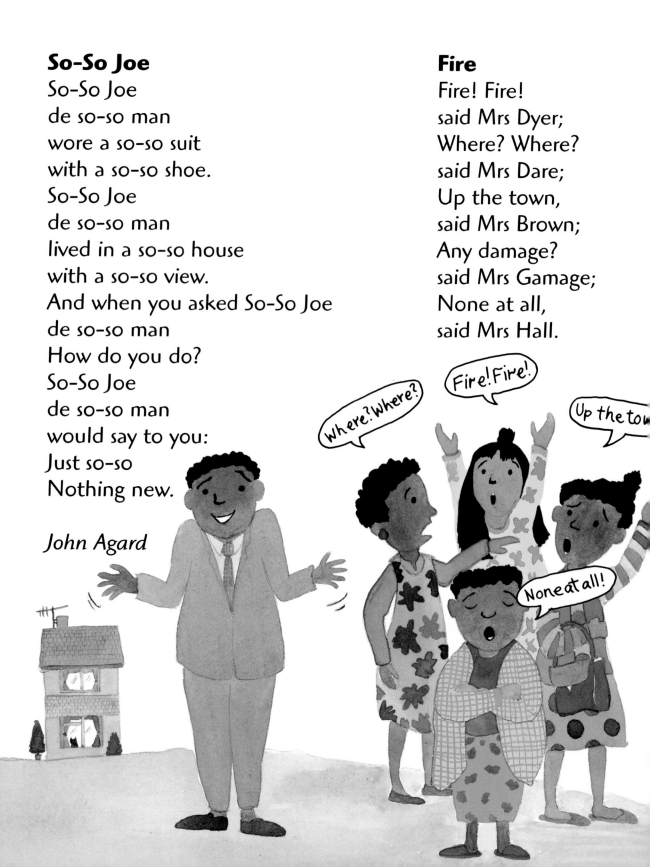

So-So Joe

So-So Joe
de so-so man
wore a so-so suit
with a so-so shoe.
So-So Joe
de so-so man
lived in a so-so house
with a so-so view.
And when you asked So-So Joe
de so-so man
How do you do?
So-So Joe
de so-so man
would say to you:
Just so-so
Nothing new.

John Agard

Fire

Fire! Fire!
said Mrs Dyer;
Where? Where?
said Mrs Dare;
Up the town,
said Mrs Brown;
Any damage?
said Mrs Gamage;
None at all,
said Mrs Hall.

The Dustman

Every Thursday morning,
Before you're quite awake,
Without the slightest warning
The house begins to shake
With a Biff! ... Bang!
Biff! Bang! Bash!

It's the dustman, who begins
(Bang! ... Crash!)
To empty both the bins
Of their rubbish and their ash,
With a Biff! ... Bang!
Biff! Bang! Bash!

Clive Sansom

The Key of the Kingdom

This is the key of the kingdom:
In that kingdom is a city,
In that city is a town,
In that town there is a street,
In that street there winds a lane,
In that lane there is a yard,
In that yard there is a house,
In that house there waits a room,
In that room there is a bed,
On that bed there is a basket,
A basket of flowers.

Flowers in the basket,
Basket on the bed,
Bed in the room,
Room in the house,
House in the weedy yard,
Yard in the winding lane,
Lane in the broad street,
Street in the high town,
Town in the city,
City in the kingdom:
This is the key of the kingdom.

Lane

Granny Granny Please Comb My Hair

Granny Granny
please comb my hair
you always take your time
you always take such care

You put me to sit on a cushion
between your knees
you rub a little coconut oil
parting gentle as a breeze

Mummy Mummy
she's always in a hurry-hurry
rush
she pulls my hair
sometimes she tugs

But Granny
you have all the time in the world
and when you're finished
you always turn my head and say
"Now who's a nice girl".

Grace Nichols

After a Bath

After my bath
I try, try, try
to wipe myself
till I'm dry, dry, dry.

Hands to wipe
and fingers and toes
and two wet legs
and a shiny nose.

Just think how much
less time I'd take
if I were a dog
and could shake, shake, shake.

Aileen Fisher

I Can Put My Socks On

I can put my socks on,
I can find my vest,
I can put my pants on –
I can't do the rest.

Tony Bradman

There Was a Young Lady Named Maggie
There was a young lady named Maggie,
Whose dog was enormous and shaggy.
    The front end of him
    Looked vicious and grim,
But the back end was friendly and waggy.

A Cheerful Old Bear at the Zoo
A cheerful old bear at the zoo,
Could always find something to do.
    When it bored him to go
    On a walk to and fro,
He reversed it and walked fro and to.

There Was a Young Farmer of Leeds

There was a young farmer of Leeds,
Who swallowed six packets of seeds.
    It soon came to pass
    He was covered with grass,
And he couldn't sit down for the weeds.

There Was a Young Man of Devizes

There was a young man of Devizes,
Whose ears were of different sizes.
    One was so small
    It was no use at all,
But the other was huge and won prizes.

I Won't

I won't, no I won't, no I won't do that.
I don't want to, I don't have to,
No I won't wear that hat.

I hate it, yes I hate it, yes I hate, hate, hate.
You can't make me, I don't want to,
I don't care if we are late.

Yes I'm naughty, yes I'm naughty,
Yes I know, know, know.
But I won't wear that hat
So it's No! No! No!

Michelle Magorian

Overheard on a Saltmarsh

Nymph, nymph, what are your beads?
Green glass, goblin. Why do you stare at them?
Give them me.
         No.
Give them me. Give them me.
         No.
Then I will howl all night in the reeds,
Lie in the mud and howl for them.
Goblin, why do you love them so?
They are better than stars or water,
Better than voices of winds that sing,
Better than any man's fair daughter,
Your green glass beads on a silver ring.

Hush, I stole them out of the moon.
Give me your beads, I desire them.
         No.
I will howl in a deep lagoon
For your green glass beads, I love them so.
Give them me. Give them.
         No.

Harold Munro

Swan, Swim over the Sea

Swan, swim over the sea.
Swim, swan, swim!
Swan, swim back again.
Well swum, swan!

"Night-night, Knight,"

"Night-night, Knight," said one Knight
to the other Knight the other night.
"Night-night, Knight."

Peter Piper Picked a Peck of Pickled Pepper

Peter Piper picked a peck of pickled pepper,
A peck of pickled pepper Peter Piper picked.
If Peter Piper picked a peck of pickled pepper,
Where's the peck of pickled pepper Peter Piper picked?

You can have

Fried fresh fish,

Fish fried fresh,

Fresh fried fish,

Fresh fish fried,

Or fish fresh fried.

Cats
Cats sleep
Anywhere,
Any table,
Any chair,
Top of piano,
Window-ledge,
In the middle,
On the edge,
Open drawer,
Empty shoe,
Anybody's
Lap will do,
Fitted in a
Cardboard box,
In the cupboard
With your frocks –
Anywhere!
They don't care!
Cats sleep
Anywhere.

Eleanor Farjeon

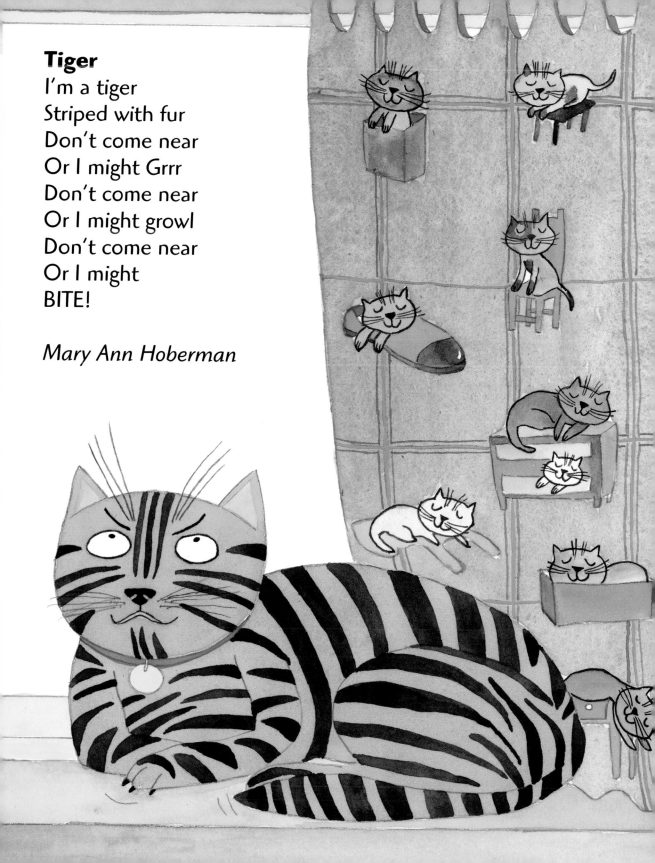

Tiger
I'm a tiger
Striped with fur
Don't come near
Or I might Grrr
Don't come near
Or I might growl
Don't come near
Or I might
BITE!

Mary Ann Hoberman

I Am Running in a Circle
I am running in a circle
and my feet are getting sore,
and my head is
spinning
spinning
as it's never spun before,
I am
dizzy
dizzy
dizzy.

NURSERY CRIMES by Michael Rosen

Hush-a-bye, Gravy, on the Tree Top

Hush-a-bye, gravy, on the tree top,
When the wind blows the ladle will rock;
When the bough breaks the ladle will fall,
Down will come gravy, ladle and all.

Humpty Dumpty Sat on the Wall

Humpty Dumpty sat on the wall,
Humpty Dumpty had a great fall;
All the King's horses and all the King's men
Trod on him.

Hey Diddle, Diddle

Hey diddle, diddle,
The cat and the fiddle,
The cow jumped over the moon;
The little dog laughed
To see such fun,
And the dish ran away with the chocolate biscuits.

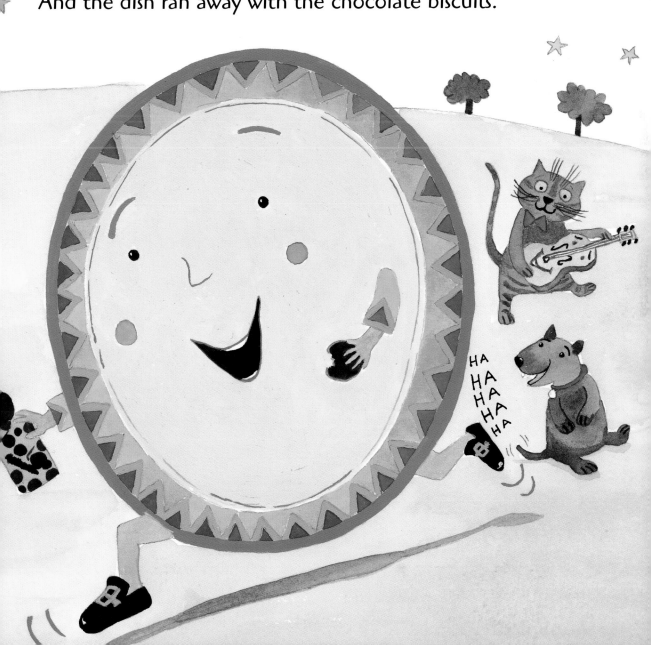

Today I Saw a Little Worm

Today I saw a little worm
Wriggling on his belly.
Perhaps he'd like to come inside
And see what's on the telly.

Spike Milligan

"Who's That Tickling My Back?"
"Who's that tickling my back?"
Said the wall.
"Me," said the caterpillar.
"I'm learning to crawl."   Ian Serraillier

Where Does Laughter Begin?
Does it start in your head
and spread to your toe?

Does it start in your cheeks
and grow downward so
till your knees feel weak?

Does it start with a tickle
in your tummy so
till you want to jump right out

of all your skin?
Or does laughter simply begin

with your mouth?

John Agard

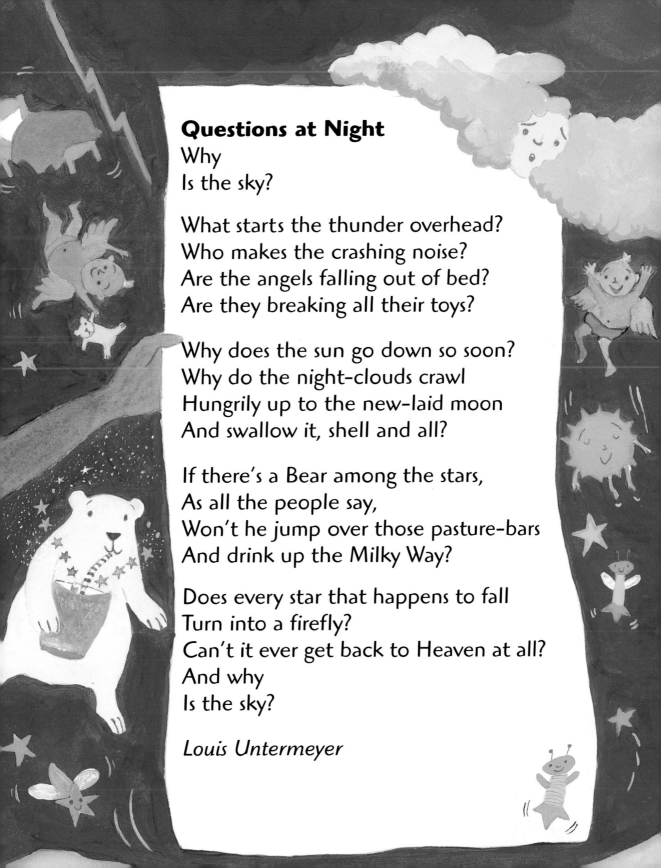

Questions at Night

Why
Is the sky?

What starts the thunder overhead?
Who makes the crashing noise?
Are the angels falling out of bed?
Are they breaking all their toys?

Why does the sun go down so soon?
Why do the night-clouds crawl
Hungrily up to the new-laid moon
And swallow it, shell and all?

If there's a Bear among the stars,
As all the people say,
Won't he jump over those pasture-bars
And drink up the Milky Way?

Does every star that happens to fall
Turn into a firefly?
Can't it ever get back to Heaven at all?
And why
Is the sky?

Louis Untermeyer

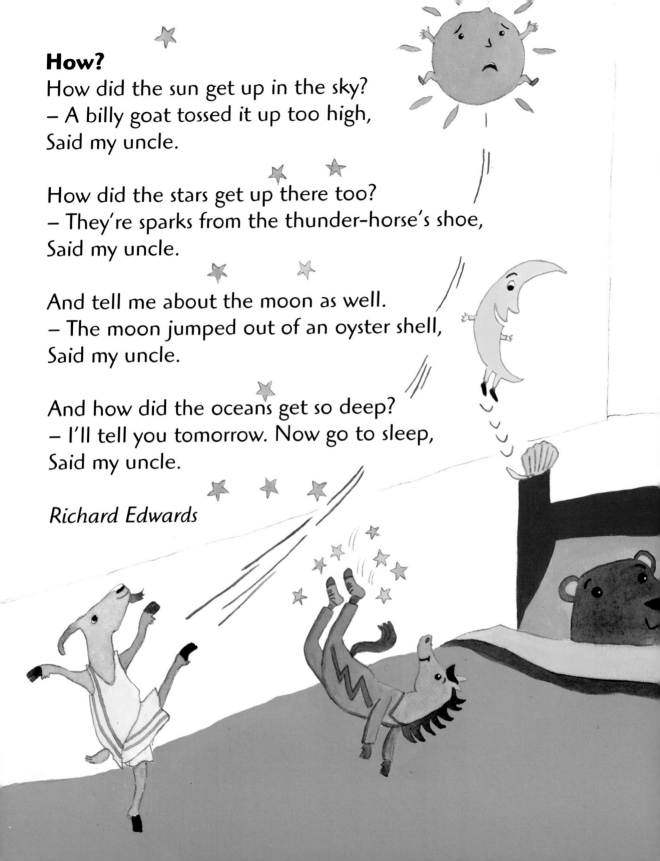

How?

How did the sun get up in the sky?
– A billy goat tossed it up too high,
Said my uncle.

How did the stars get up there too?
– They're sparks from the thunder-horse's shoe,
Said my uncle.

And tell me about the moon as well.
– The moon jumped out of an oyster shell,
Said my uncle.

And how did the oceans get so deep?
– I'll tell you tomorrow. Now go to sleep,
Said my uncle.

Richard Edwards

Silverly

Silverly,
      Silverly
Over the
      Trees,
The moon drifts
      By on a
Runaway
      Breeze.

Dozily,
      Dozily
Deep in her
      Bed,
A little girl
      Dreams with the
Moon in her
      Head.

Dennis Lee

MORE WALKER PAPERBACKS
For You to Enjoy

A CUP OF STARSHINE
compiled by Jill Bennett, illustrated by Graham Percy

In this lively anthology for young children you'll find poems about subjects as diverse as washing and springtime, playing and the moon…

"A beautifully produced and illustrated anthology." *Independent on Sunday*

0-7445-6097-7   £6.99

ASANA AND THE ANIMALS
by Grace Nichols / Sarah Adams

This book sings with the rhymes of a little girl called Asana, who celebrates the animals that she knows and likes and dreams about – from a caterpillar to a Jersey cow, a hedgehog to a jogging ocelot, a giraffe to her grandmother's cat!

"All the poems read aloud well and will prompt lively discussion." *The School Librarian*

0-7445-5498-5   £5.99

TEA IN THE SUGAR BOWL, POTATO IN MY SHOE
by Michael Rosen / Quentin Blake

Beginning with the chaos of breakfast and ending with the calm of bedtime, this quirky collection is full of delightful moments. Read of the pleasures of messing about and the pains of feeling ill, of animal antics down at the doctor's and strange goings-on at the beach… All this and a trip on a flying bed, too!

"Lots of zany humour and illustrations by the excellent Quentin Blake… Lots of fun." *Tony Bradman, Parents*

0-7445-5438-1   £4.99